TOOWOOMBA REGIONAL LIBRARY SERVICES

a passion for
coffee

a passion for
coffee

hattie ellis

photography by debi treloar

RYLAND
PETERS
& SMALL
LONDON NEW YORK

Designer Jo Fernandes
Senior Editor Clare Double
Picture Research Emily Westlake
Production Eleanor Cant
Art Director Anne-Marie Bulat
Publishing Director Alison Starling
Stylist Emily Chalmers
Food Stylist Fiona Smith

First published in the United Kingdom in 2006
by Ryland Peters & Small
20–21 Jockey's Fields
London WC1R 4BW
www.rylandpeters.com

10 9 8 7 6 5 4 3 2 1
Text, design and commissioned photographs
© Ryland Peters & Small 2002, 2006
A longer version of this text was previously
published in *Coffee* (2002).

ISBN-10: 1-84597-229-5
ISBN-13: 978-1-84597-229-5
Printed and bound in China

contents

Coffea arabica

Opposite, clockwise from top left *Freshly ground coffee; Colombian beans; very dark roasted beans; green beans; Kibo Chagga beans from Tanzania; Middle Eastern coffee with cardamom seeds.*

what is coffee?

Coffee beans begin life as the seeds inside the cherries of an evergreen plant, *Coffea arabica*, which grows in the humid lands between the tropic of Cancer and the tropic of Capricorn. They range from fruity Kenyans to chocolatey Guatemalans, from spicy Indonesians to clean Costa Ricans.

After the cherries are harvested their outer layers are removed and the green beans found within travel around the globe. Roasted, ground and mixed with hot water, the beans' concentrated, aromatic flavours are released to make one of the most remarkable and celebrated drinks in the world. Transformed from

plant to cup, the tastes – of lemon, of blueberries, of wine – that lie within this bitter black brew can still remind you of its origins at the heart of a fruit.

Ancient as tribes and irrepressibly modern, coffee adapts itself to time and place, encompassing the romantic, the industrious and the day-to-day. Its dynamic history is full of tales of passion and intrigue, yet it is also the everyday drink of breakfast and of mid-morning office breaks. Prized for its intriguing range of flavours and styles, used as a digestive, and relied upon as a stimulant, coffee excites and focuses the brain along with the rest of the body. It brings us together over cups and conversation. Its aromatic allure can beckon us away from our daily business to a café for a quiet sip, a newspaper and a view of the world. Solitary or sociable, it allows us both to unwind and to recharge.

The current surge of interest in coffee has developed through a growing awareness of the quality end of the market, in freshly roasted beans that have a particular provenance and a distinctive taste, and in the many ways of drinking coffee, such as cappuccino and espresso. A *Passion for Coffee* celebrates coffee in all its forms and looks at how to discover and enjoy its many flavours.

the buzz

the origins of coffee

Ethiopia, believed by many to be the ancient birthplace of mankind, is where coffee's long history begins. Legend tells of Kaldi, a goatherd in Abyssinia who noticed his animals prancing around after nibbling at the leaves and fruit of particular bushes. So right from the start, the plant was recognized and prized as a stimulant. Monks took coffee to keep them awake for nocturnal prayers, and travellers rolled the cherries with fat into balls to make an early trail food.

Coffea arabica was cultivated by the Arabs, who used coffee both as a medicine and as a pleasurable stimulant. Coffee houses sprang up where people met to drink, play backgammon, talk, and listen to music and storytelling. Pilgrims and traders spread the bean around the Muslim world, and its fame – and consumption – spanned North Africa, Turkey and Persia.

Coffee houses came to be regarded as subversive – as places of temptation and ideological ferment – but the drink's progress around the world was indefatigable, as people discovered this *qahwa al-bon*, 'wine of the bean', that could waken mind, spirit and senses.

spread around the world

Coffee consumption took off in the West in the 17th century. One of the bean's early European destinations was the trade centre of Venice, which received coffee with other goods from the East. At first, Christian leaders rejected the drink as darkly satanic. However, once Pope Clement VIII took a sip, he blessed the new brew as heavenly instead.

Coffee houses popularized the drink wherever it was consumed. Coinciding with the founding of newspapers and the thinking of the Enlightenment, coffee became known as the drink of democracy. British coffee houses were called 'penny universities' because, for the price of a cup, people could meet and discuss politics and philosophy.

The first French café, Café Procope, opened its doors opposite the Comédie Française in 1689, and soon became the haunt of philosophers, writers and political activists. By the end of the 18th century there were 800 cafés in Paris and by 1843 there were 3,000.

After the Boston Tea Party, Americans saw tea as unpatriotic and became a nation of coffee drinkers. The bean, now grown outside Africa and Arabia, arrived on the doorstep of the booming US market in Latin America, which was to become the world's biggest producer of coffee.

coffee trade

Coffee grows on vast Brazilian plantations and is collected from the wild in Ethiopian forests; it is cultivated on ancient terraces carved into the mountainsides of Yemen and on Indonesian smallholdings. In volume, coffee is the second most traded commodity in the world, after oil.

Coffee production can be affected by political upheaval, when growers may switch from export crops to subsistence farming, and it is prone to the natural disasters such as hurricanes and floods that can devastate the tropics. Global price fluctuations can mean bankruptcy to the small grower, which is why the Fairtrade movement (see page 63) guarantees a stable price that goes directly to the producer and enables them to continue farming in a sustainable way.

Some of the best coffees end up in specialist coffee merchants. They have the experience and contacts to source consistently good beans from the market, tasting each new crop and roasting every batch of beans to perfection to bring out their optimum flavours. To find them, just follow the tantalizing aromas that wisp out from a good coffee shop or café.

famous coffee drinkers

Coffee gives people energy, and cafés bring them together – a potent combination. Voltaire downed as many as 50 cups a day. Beethoven would count 60 beans into a single cup. Balzac walked across Paris to get three kinds of coffee from different shops to make a blend that kept him awake to write from midnight until midday. He explained that when he drank coffee, '… ideas begin to move … the paper is covered in ink.'

The Boston Tea Party was planned in secrecy at the Green Dragon coffee house. And, just a few years later in 1789, Desmoulins whipped up a revolutionary crowd when he leapt onto a table to speak from the Café Foy in Paris; two days later, the Bastille was stormed.

'Strong coffee, and plenty, awakens me,' said Napoleon, who favoured a Brazilian Santos-Mocha blend. 'It gives me warmth, an unusual force, a pain that is not without pleasure.'

Jean-Paul Sartre and Simone de Beauvoir wrote at Les Deux Magots, a Left Bank café, while the Beat Poets drank coffee and talked the talk at the Caffe Trieste and the Co-Existence Bagel Shop in San Francisco. Impressionism, Surrealism, Cubism, Existentialism – all these movements were brewed in the atmosphere of cafés and coffee shops.

the beans

understanding terms

Arabica beans, from *Coffea arabica*, are the coffee connoisseur's choice. The plant grows best at higher altitudes, and its slowly grown, hard beans have more flavour than coffees from the more easily grown *Coffea robusta* beans. Look also for coffee labelled 'high grown' or 'hard bean'.

Older varieties of the arabica coffee plant, such as Bourbon, are worth seeking out. So, too, are specialities such as Peaberry coffee, which comes from cherries with a single, rounder bean, and the large Maragogype, or 'elephant' beans, which are prized both for their appearance and their smooth taste.

The way in which the beans are separated from their surrounding pulp also plays a part in the character of the coffee in your cup. Wet-processed, or washed, beans tend to have lighter, subtle flavours, while the dry-processed beans, from areas where water is in short supply, can have an earthy, fruity character.

When tasting coffee, notice the aroma and the flavours inside the cup; the body, which is the feel of the coffee in your mouth, cleanly light to lusciously full; and its acidity, which spreads across your tongue and lifts the drink by providing an additional, lively layer of enjoyment.

roasts and blends

Coffee is exported as green beans. These are sent around the world in sacks, and are then roasted by specialists to bring out their subtle flavours. As the beans heat up and turn a glossy brown, the oils that are the secret of their marvellous flavour develop.

Roasts vary from light brown through medium to the very dark beans favoured by the French and Italians. Light roasts, such as 'cinnamon', have a more delicate, mildly aromatic taste. Medium roasts, also known as 'city' or 'American', are slightly stronger. Viennese roasts are a little darker still than medium, while French, Italian and Continental roasts edge into deep brown and near-black, producing enticingly bitter, richly pungent flavours, such as those found in Italian espresso.

The art of blending is to marry different beans together to create a harmonious balance of flavours, acidity and body. Specialist coffee merchants pride themselves on their variations on classics, such as mellow breakfast blends, stronger after-dinner blends and those used to make espresso. One long-standing combination is Mocha-Java, which combines aroma and strength to make a delicious, potent brew. It takes skill and constant tasting to create and maintain house blends, as even beans from the same place will vary from batch to batch and from year to year.

the Americas

Since the plant was first cultivated commercially on the continent in the 18th century, the Americas have become the largest producers of coffee in the world. Costa Rican beans are highly prized for their fragrance, balance and entrancing acidity. Tarrazu is the most famous region in a land known as the Switzerland of coffee countries for its consistency, clean flavours and attention to detail. This is a good place to source high-altitude beans, such as the high-grade Strictly Hard Bean (SHB).

For a contrast in style, the rugged terrain and remote highlands of Guatemala produce smoky, chocolatey, fruity beans loved for their distinctive individuality. Look out for beans such as those from Huehuetenango, the volcanic slopes above the city of Antigua and the moist climate of Cobán.

Brazil grows around a third of the world's coffee, much of it on vast plantations. Specialists hunt out high-grade Brazilian coffees, such as those from the older Bourbon plant. Colombia, the second largest coffee producer in the world, is known for the full-bodied, mellow consistency of its washed coffees, from the *supremo* (large) to *excelso* (smaller) beans.

Mexico produces nutty beans with Central American acidity, and is known for its extra-large Maragogype beans. Hawaii has the smooth, complex Kona coffees, and Jamaica's Blue Mountain is famous for its high-quality beans, which command equally high prices.

Africa

Some coffee grows wild in its indigenous home of Ethiopia, and the beans produced from this ancient land intrigue drinkers with their winey, gamey, perfumed flavours and aromatic hints of apricots, blueberries, lemon, grapes and flowers. Look out for coffees such as those from Harrar and from the Sidamo region, which may be labelled after the town of Yirgacheffe. Likely to be grown without pesticides or artificial fertilizers, the natural wildness of these plants translates into the cup as rare, interesting coffees.

Across the Red Sea, Yemeni coffees share some of the same characteristics and may be called Mocha, after the port that exported early coffees to Europe. These beans of Arabia can be perfumed with a heavy-bodied piquancy and a bright acidity. Dry-processed, they can be earthy with an almost liquorice tang. Mattari and Sanani coffees are the best known.

Grown high up, some at over 1,500 metres (5,000 feet), Kenyan coffees can stop you in your tracks with their pure, fresh, tangy tastes. Kenyan beans are loved for their balance of beautiful body, clean acidity and berry fruitiness. The top-grade beans are graded AA, and are wet-processed. Kenyan Peaberries, with their single fruit, are a speciality and have a satisfyingly rounded appearance and a smooth, sometimes malty, taste.

Tanzania, Zimbabwe and Malawi can all grow coffee with the sparkling acidity and fruitiness of the East African style.

Asia

The Dutch first grew coffee on the Indonesian island of Java, and its name has been used to refer to all the coffees from this country and, historically, for coffee in general. Javanese coffees are known for their earthy, spicy, rich flavours. Sumatra and Sulawesi also grow luscious, full-bodied coffees with strong, distinctive flavours of herbs, woods, spices and even syrupy-smooth caramel. Sulawesi coffees are sometimes sold under the former Dutch name for the island, Celebes.

One intriguing, and expensive, Indonesian speciality is the Kopi Luak coffee, made from beans eaten and excreted by a small, cat-like wild animal, the luak. The beans, transformed in the animal's digestive tract, have, as you might imagine, something of a cult following. Some Indonesian coffees are aged to mimic the taste acquired when the beans were stockpiled in the islands' damp, warm climate or underwent long sea voyages to the West. Neighbouring Papua New Guinea produces coffees with a perfumed tropical fruitiness.

Coffee has been grown in India since the 17th century and specialities include aged Monsoon coffees, where the beans are exposed to the monsoon winds in open warehouses. The result is a coffee with a special, mellow flavour. Southern India grows coffees with enticing scents of spices. Mysore coffees are one kind known for quality, as they come from a state where arabica plants are grown.

flavoured coffee

Certain flavours have an affinity with coffee, hence the chocolate on the top of a cappuccino or the spoonful of vanilla sugar added to an after-dinner cup. Spiced coffees are traditional in the Middle East, where the grounds may be mixed with cardamom and other flavours such as cinnamon, nutmeg and cloves. On parts of the Amalfi coast in Italy, they sometimes add a twist of peel from their famous lemons, and the habit has followed some Italians living in America. Modern flavoured coffees use essential oils to make such brews as pecan nut and raspberries and cream. You can also buy or make flavoured sugar syrups to add to brewed coffees (orange is a good one), or add a dash of a liqueur for a tasty kick.

decaffeinated coffee

Decaffeinated coffees are made by dissolving the caffeine out of the beans using chemical solvents or water. Look for decaf sold by people who care about quality. Some of the taste disappears with the caffeine, so the coffee must be made from beans with plenty of flavour in the first place. Lesser merchants use cheap, less delicious beans to compensate for the cost of the decaffeination process, which is why the drink can taste underpowered in more than one sense. Robusta coffees, incidentally, contain about twice as much caffeine as the higher-quality arabicas.

the brew

buying and storing

Coffee becomes much more interesting if you buy it from a specialist retailer. You can purchase through the internet and by mail order, or steep yourself in the sensory delight of the shop itself with all its aromas and busy sounds: the grinding, the chinking, the shake, rattle and roll of the beans. A good retailer will have a wide choice of high-quality beans; they may do their own roasting, and will be able to give you advice on what to try.

Freshness is the key to good coffee. The aromatic oils start to disappear immediately after roasting so it is best to buy small amounts of freshly roasted beans regularly, instead of a large amount in one go. Buy coffee as you would other fresh foods, and use it at its peak. When beans are freshly roasted, the grounds tend to foam up when you add water.

For best results, buy whole beans and grind them at home just before brewing, as the oils lose their volatile aromas even more quickly once the coffee is ground. A specialist retailer will also grind beans for you. An inexpensive propeller-blade grinder is a good way to start, or pay more for a burr grinder, which mills the coffee between discs to get a more even grind and has settings that can be adjusted for different grades from coarse to fine.

Coffee should be stored in an airtight, dry container, in a cool cupboard rather than in the fridge. You can also freeze beans in an airtight bag for a couple of months, and grind them while still frozen.

secrets of the perfect cup

These four principles make all the difference between insipid meekness or brutish bitterness and what you want in coffee – aromatic energy.

• Buy freshly roasted, good-quality beans and grind just before brewing.

• Make sure the grind is right for the method you are using.

• Measure the coffee and water you need and the brewing time. Using the correct proportion of coffee to water and letting them brew together for the right duration means you extract maximum character and aromatic oils from the beans without the brew becoming bitter. For weaker coffee, it is better to add hot water to properly brewed coffee than to use too much water or too few beans.

• With the exception of Middle Eastern coffee, which is boiled, pour the water onto the grounds when it is just off the boil. This dissolves the soluble flavours from the coffee without scalding the subtleties into bitterness. Do not keep coffee warm on the heat or it will become bitter.

espresso know-how

Espresso is made by forcing hot water through finely ground, dark-roasted coffee under pressure so that it blasts through the grounds, extracting maximum flavour.

At home, Italians often make espressos in a stove-top pot; the Moka is the classic model. Fill the bottom half with water up to the rivet on the side and fill the coffee container to the brim with finely ground coffee, levelling it gently so the water can get through evenly. Screw the top tightly onto the bottom. When the coffee is ready, you will hear air bubbling through the connecting tube, once all the water has gone through.

If you want to buy an espresso machine go for one that provides high pressure, such as a pump-action model, to get most flavour. Expensive versions approach the engineering of those used in cafés. You can also buy machines with ready-to-use coffee pods, but this restricts your choice and the beans are not freshly ground.

filters, cafetières and more

All these methods require 2 tablespoons of coffee per 180 ml water and need to brew for 4–6 minutes to extract the beans' fullest flavour.

• The popular plunge-pot, or cafetière, uses coarsely ground coffee. Give the coffee a stir once you have poured on the water. Infuse for 4 minutes. You can wrap a tea towel around the pot to keep the liquid hot while brewing, or use an insulated plunge-pot.

• When making filter coffee, wet the medium-fine ground coffee first with a little hot water to help the water filter through evenly.

• Old-fashioned French drip pots work on the same principle as filter coffee and come in three parts: a pot, a filter with holes, and a top section with a lid. You put medium ground coffee in the filter, pour water into the top part and let it drip through to the bottom.

• Recently revived, the vacuum-pot method requires a medium-fine grind and produces coffee with a beautiful clarity of flavour.

milk and sugar?

Milk goes with coffee in many delicious ways. Hot milk works better than cold: French waiters will simultaneously pour a jet of coffee from one pot and hot milk from another to form a *café au lait*; an Italian 'stains' an espresso with a drop of steamed milk to make *caffè macchiato* or adds it, half and half, to make a latte.

Milk softens and alters flavours. When trying a new bean, taste the coffee black first, then add milk and judge how its character is altered. Cream also adds smoothness to a cup.

Sugar takes away some of the bitterness in coffee, though well-made coffee should have only a subtle edge of bitterness. You may like to add a spoonful to dark-roasted coffee, such as espresso, but not to lighter styles. Eating cakes or biscuits with your coffee is, of course, an excellent way to sweeten the moment.

cappuccino, latte and au lait...

The classic cappuccino is made using one third espresso, one third steamed milk and one third foam. Espresso machines usually have a metal wand which steams and froths the milk. Alternatively, heat milk in a saucepan or microwave and then whisk it by hand until it froths. You can also buy electric milk-frothing whisks, some of which come with containers that go in the microwave to heat the milk. Pour the hot milk onto the coffee, holding back the froth with a spoon, and add the frothed milk last. If desired, top off the cappuccino with powdered chocolate.

You can also drink a *cappuccino senza schiuma* (without foam); a *cappuccino chiaro*, with less coffee and more milk; or the darker *cappuccino scuro*, which contains less milk. Just use your eye and your tastebuds to judge the proportions.

A *caffè latte* is made from roughly half hot or steamed milk and half espresso mixed together. The French *café au lait* is the same, except that it is made with filter coffee.

café society

There are many reasons for coffee's popularity, from the medical to the gastronomic, but at base its appeal is that the caffeine it contains is quickly absorbed into the bloodstream, providing a hit of mental alertness. Different countries have evolved places where people can drink and take a break, from the zinc-topped counters of French cafés and the wood-panelled sophistication of the Viennese coffee house to the bright zap of the modern coffee chain. Café society is about people meeting, thinking, writing, talking – or simply taking time out with a coffee brew.

Italian coffee drinking

Hot shots of coffee fuel the animated Italians. Cappuccino is a milky breakfast brew that may be drunk with a *cornetto* (croissant). The drink, with its hood of frothed milk, is named after the colour of Capuchin monks' habits. The monks themselves were named after their own hoods (*cappuccio*).

The classic espresso is a very short measure – just a few long, deliciously bitter sips – and a well-made one has a pale brown foam, or *crema*, on top. A *caffè doppio* is a double measure. *Caffè lungo* has more water for a milder drink and *caffè ristretto* has less water for a stronger brew. A *caffè macchiato* contains a dollop of steamed milk, while a *latte macchiato* is milk with a drop of coffee.

On hot days, you can refresh yourself with a *caffè freddo* (iced coffee) or a *caffè latte freddo*, with milk. And on a cold day, or after dinner, you could add a drop of spirits for a fortifying *caffè corretto*.

Middle Eastern coffee

An *ibrik*, or *kanaka*, is the tapered pot with a long handle and a pouring lip used in the Middle Eastern method of boiling coffee with water. Mix one or two heaped teaspoons of very, very finely ground coffee with an equal amount of sugar for each demitasse (little cup) of water. The *ibrik* must be only half full, as the mixture will expand as it boils. Bring to the boil over a medium heat, then reduce the heat to low. Bring to the boil again, then turn the heat off. (Alternatively, you can repeat the boiling once more at this stage, if desired.)

Half fill the cups with coffee, then add some of the prized foam to the top of each drink. For an extra-aromatic brew, use Middle Eastern coffee that is ready-mixed with cardamom.

spiced orange coffee syrup

10 green cardamom pods

250 g sugar

125 ml strong coffee or espresso

1 teaspoon finely grated orange zest

1 cinnamon stick, broken into pieces

serves 6–8

A syrup for ice cream spiced with the cardamom that often flavours Middle Eastern coffee.

Crush the cardamom pods with a knife and scrape out the seeds. Put the sugar into a heavy-bottomed saucepan, add 60 ml water and heat very slowly until the sugar dissolves – gently draw a spoon across the sugar to help the process. When all the sugar has dissolved, boil for 2 minutes, then stir in the coffee, orange zest, cinnamon and cardamom. Let cool so the flavours infuse, then strain and store the syrup in an airtight jar in the refrigerator.

To serve, pour over vanilla or chocolate ice cream.

coffee and alcohol

Coffee is often served at the end of a meal and
it combines beautifully with spirits, either
drunk alongside one another, or in the same
cup. To make Irish coffee, pour Irish whiskey
(other spirits work well, too) into a glass with
a spoonful of sugar, add strong, hot coffee and
pour on double cream over a spoon so it floats
on top. Alternatively, simply add a drop of
brandy, Calvados, grappa or another liqueur
to black or white coffee for an extra glow of
heat. Rum and orange-flavoured liqueurs
such as Cointreau work particularly well

iced coffee

2 tablespoons ground coffee

4 ice cubes

1 small scoop vanilla or chocolate ice cream (optional)

125 ml milk

1 teaspoon sugar, or to taste

a dash of liqueur (optional)

serves 1

You can add a splash of a liqueur such as Cointreau or rum to this deliciously refreshing drink.

Brew the coffee using your normal method, but make it stronger than usual (using 125 ml water with the 2 tablespoons ground coffee) because it will be diluted by the ice cubes. When brewed, pour the coffee over the ice cubes. As an extra touch, you can put a small scoop of ice cream on the ice cubes before you pour over the coffee. Stir in the milk, sugar and liqueur, if using.

Serve immediately or chill until required.

useful addresses

Angelucci
23b Frith Street
London W1D 4RT
020 7437 5889

Algerian Coffee Stores
52 Old Compton Street
London W1D 4PB
020 7437 2480
www.algcoffee.co.uk
Open since 1887, specialist
suppliers of tea and coffee.
Wide range of coffee-making
equipment.

Aroma Tea and Coffee Merchants
8a St Marys Place
Shrewsbury SY1 1DZ
01743 367598
www.aroma-coffee.co.uk

Better Beverage Company
204 Morrison Street
Edinburgh EH3 8EA
0131 4762600
www.betterbeverage.co.uk

The Bramah Tea and Coffee Museum
40 Southwark Street
London SE1 1UN
020 7403 5650
www.bramahmuseum.co.uk

Camden Coffee Stores
11 Delancey Street
London NW1 7NL
020 7387 4080

Coffee Plant
180 Portobello Road
London W11 2EB
020 7221 8137
www.coffee.uk.com

The Drury Tea and Coffee Company
3 New Row
London WC2N 4LH
020 7836 1960
www.drury.uk.com

Farrers
13 Stricklandgate
Kendal LA9 4LY
01539 731707
www.farrers.com

Gillards of Bath
55 Guildhall Market
Bath BA2 4AW
01225 311888
www.gillards.co.uk

H. R. Higgins (Coffee-Man) Ltd
79 Duke Street
London W1K 5AS
020 7629 3913
www.hrhiggins.co.uk

Imperial Teas and Coffees
26 Steep Hill
Lincoln LN2 1LU
01522 560008
www.imperialteas.co.uk

Layton Fern & Co. Ltd
27 Rathbone Place
London W1T 1EP
020 7636 2237
www.laytonfern.fsnet.co.uk

Love Saves the Day
345 Deansgate
Knott Hill
Manchester M3 4LG
0161 8342266
www.lovesavestheday.co.uk

Markus Coffee Company
13 Connaught Street
London W2 2AY
020 7723 4020

W. Martyn
135 Muswell Hill Broadway
London N10 3RS
020 8883 5642

Mecca Tea and Coffee Merchants
25 Chalybeate Street
Aberystwyth SY23 1HX
01970 612888

Monmouth Coffee Company
27 Monmouth Street
London WC2H 9DD
020 7379 3516
2 Park Street
London SE1 9AB
020 7645 3585
www.monmouthcoffee.co.uk
Coffee roasters and retailers.

Steamer Trading Cookshop
20–21 High Street
Lewes
East Sussex BN7 2LN
01273 487230
www.steamer.co.uk
And branches.

Wilkinson's of Norwich
5 Lobster Lane
Norwich NR2 1DQ
01603 625121
www.wilkinsonsofnorwich.com

Fairtrade movement

Cafédirect
City Cloisters, Suite B2
196 Old Street
London EC1V 9FR
020 7490 9520
www.cafedirect.co.uk

Thanks to the following for the
loan of props for photography.

Muji
6–17 Tottenham Court Road
London W1P 9DP
020 7436 1779
www.muji.co.uk
Practical and stylish household
items from Japan.

David Mellor
4 Sloane Square
London SW1W 8EE
020 7730 4259
www.davidmellordesign.co.uk
Specialists in award-winning
cutlery and fine kitchenware.

Helena Rohner
c/Almendro 4
Madrid 28005, Spain
00 34 91 36 57 906
Handcrafted tableware in
ceramic and wood.

The Conran Shop
Michelin House
81 Fulham Road
London SW3 6RD
020 7589 7401
www.conranshop.co.uk
Design-led home and
kitchenware.

After Noah
121 Upper Street
London N1 1QP
020 7359 4281
www.afternoah.com
Vintage and contemporary
kitchen and home ware.

Immaculate House
Old Spitalfields Market
57 Brushfield Street
London E1 6AA
020 7375 1844

Fortnum and Mason
181 Piccadilly
London W1A 1ER
020 7734 8040
www.fortnumandmason.co.uk
Specialist tea and coffee.

Bowles and Linares
32 Hereford Road
London W2 5AJ
020 7229 9886
www.bowlesandlinares.co.uk
Coffee filters, jugs, cups and
saucers made from clear and
amber coloured glass.

Nicole Farhi Home
17 Clifford Street
London W1X 8BY
020 7494 9051
www.nicolefarhi.com
Old and new home wares.

To Clare Moberly

picture credits

All photographs by Debi Treloar except the following:

William Lingwood
Pages 56, 57, 59

James Merrell
Pages 34, 38 below right, 55

David Brittain
Page 3

Peter Cassidy
Page 54

Christopher Drake
Page 51 right

Diana Miller
Page 2

Ian Wallace
Page 33

Polly Wreford
Pages 4–5

Francesca Yorke
Endpapers

PUBLISHER'S ACKNOWLEDGMENTS
The publisher would like to thank the
Monmouth Coffee Company, H. R. Higgins
(Coffee-Man) Ltd and Layton Fern & Co. Ltd
for allowing us to photograph in their premises.